Celebrating Birth
Around the World

Anita Ganeri

heinemann
raintree

Edited by Clare Lewis and Brenda Haugen
Designed by Richard Parker
Picture research by Gina Kammer
Production by Helen McCreath
Originated by Capstone Global Library Ltd
Printed and bound in China by CTPS

19 18 17 16 15
10 9 8 7 6 5 4 3 2 1

Library of Congress Cataloging-in-Publication Data
Ganeri, Anita, 1961-
  Celebrating birth around the world / Anita Ganeri.
    pages cm.—(Cultures and customs)
  Includes bibliographical references and index.
  ISBN 978-1-4109-8015-1 (hb)—ISBN 978-1-4109-8020-5 (pb)—ISBN 978-1-4109-8030-4 (ebook) 1. Childbirth—Cross-cultural studies—Juvenile literature. 2. Birth customs—Cross-cultural studies—Juvenile literature. I. Title.
  GN482.1.G36 2016
  618.4—dc23   2015000286

Acknowledgments
We would like to thank the following for permission to reproduce photographs:
Alamy: © Aurora Photos, 22, © Dan Leeth, 20, © E.R. Degginger, 21, © Godong, 8, © Horizons WWP, 13, © Tim Gainey, 7, © World Religions Photo Library, 14; AP Photo: Amr Nabil, 16, 17; Capstone Press (map), throughout; Capstone Studio: Karon Dubke, 28, 29; Corbis: © Gideon Mendel, 6; Dreamstime: © Birgit Korber, 19, © Zkruger, 10; iStockphoto: brittak, cover, CEFutcher, 5, xuanhuongho, 25; Newscom: CNImaging/Juan Cheng, 11, DanitaDelimont.com "Danita Delimont Photography"/Angel Wynn, 23, Heiner Heine imageBROKER, 18, Ingram Publishing, 12, IP3 PRESS/MAXPPP/Guillaume BONNEFONT, 24, REUTERS/BAZUKI MUHAMMAD, 15; Robert Harding: Annie Owen, 9; Shutterstock: Olesya Feketa, 26, Rob Marmion, 27

We would like to thank Dr. Suzanne Owen for her invaluable help in the preparation of this book.

Every effort has been made to contact copyright holders of material reproduced in this book. Any omissions will be rectified in subsequent printings if notice is given to the publisher.

Contents

Some words are shown in bold, **like this**. You can find out what they mean by looking in the glossary.

Celebrating
Birth

In cultures around the world, important events in people's lives are marked with special customs and ceremonies. They help people to celebrate occasions, such as the birth of a baby, a wedding, or remembering people after they have died. They are also a way to guide people from one stage of their lives to the next. This book looks at how people from different cultures and religions welcome a new baby into the world.

Many ceremonies and traditions focus on giving the baby a name. Naming a baby is a very important event. A name can show a person's family, culture, and religion, so it needs to be chosen carefully. Some naming ceremonies take place at the time of the birth itself; others happen weeks or even months later.

NEW WAYS

Some people have religious ceremonies to welcome a new baby. Other people do not follow a religion. **Humanists** do not pray to a god, but have their own ways of celebrating birth. They hold their own naming ceremonies, with music, readings, and poems. The parents introduce the baby to their friends and family and announce the baby's name.

Some babies may be named after relatives, friends, or even celebrities. Many names have meanings. What does your name mean?

Honey and Horoscopes

When a **Hindu** baby is born, a special ceremony is held. The baby is bathed, and the syllable "Om" is written on his or her tongue in honey. Om is a sacred sound in the Hindu religion. It is said at the beginning and end of prayers and blessings.

A priest writes down the time, date, and place of the baby's birth and figures out the baby's **horoscope**. From this, he gives the family three letters, and they choose a name that starts with one of them. Many Hindu babies are named after Hindu gods and goddesses. After 40 days, the baby is taken to the **mandir** for his or her naming ceremony. The priest announces the baby's name and says blessings for a long life and good health.

These Hindu parents are holding a naming ceremony for their baby. The priest is praying.

A Hindu baby's first haircut is an important time in his or her young life.

FIRST HAIRCUT

When a Hindu baby is a year old, his or her hair is completely shaved off. This is believed to take away any bad **karma** from the baby's past so that he or she can make a fresh start in life.

Another ceremony is held when the baby is six months old. This is when the baby is given his or her first taste of cooked rice.

Sacred Names

A few weeks after a **Sikh** baby's birth, the baby's parents take him or her to the **gurdwara**. They are joined by their friends and family for a naming ceremony.

In the gurdwara, the parents stand in front of the Guru Granth Sahib, the Sikhs' holy book. The **granthi** opens the book at random and reads the first word on the left-hand page. The parents choose a name that begins with the first letter of that word. They add "Singh" ("lion") as a last name if the baby is a boy and "Kaur" ("princess") for a girl.

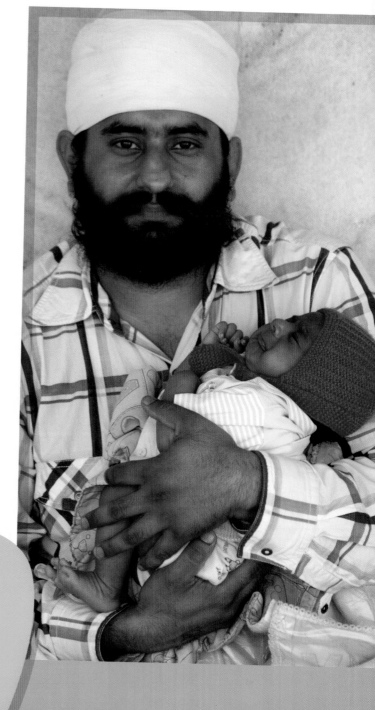

A Sikh baby's naming ceremony takes place in the gurdwara.

The Guru Granth Sahib is covered in a beautiful romalla cloth.

Afterward, everyone is given karah prasad to celebrate. This is a sweet dish made from flour, **semolina**, sugar, and butter. The baby's parents also present a romalla to the gurdwara. A romalla is a beautiful silk cloth that is used to cover the Guru Granth Sahib.

THE MOOL MANTAR

When a Sikh baby is born, the words of the Mool Mantar prayer are whispered in his or her ear:

"God is one
Whose name is Truth
God the creator
is without fear
is without hate
is timeless and without shape
is beyond death, the enlightened one
and is understood through God's grace."

Red Eggs and Ginger

When a Chinese baby is first born, the parents often give him or her a "fake" name to trick evil spirits into leaving the baby alone. The baby's real "adult" name is often picked by his or her grandparents. Sometimes babies are given their adult names right away.

When the baby is about a month old, a naming ceremony is held. This is when the baby is given a permanent name. It is called a "Red egg and ginger party." The parents send out invitations. In the past, people sent each guest a hard-boiled egg. The eggs are dyed red, which is a lucky color. Today, red eggs are placed on a table at the party for guests to take home, along with a piece of ginger. In return, the guests bring gifts of clothes for the baby or money in lucky red envelopes.

Guests take home a red egg as a sign of luck.

To thank guests for their gifts, the baby's parents send small, round pastries filled with pork, instead of thank-you notes.

At about one year old, the baby is shown a tray of objects, such as paint brushes, tools, cooking pots, or money. Whatever the baby grasps is said to show what sort of job he or she may do in adulthood.

This baby is banging a drum. Perhaps he will become a musician!

Special Food Around the World

> In South Korea, different types of rice cakes are eaten at celebrations such as birthdays, weddings, and New Year.

Rice cakes

In South Korea, special kinds of rice cakes are eaten when a baby is 100 days old. If steamed rice cakes are shared with 100 people, it is said to bring long life. So, rice cakes are sent out to as many friends and neighbors as possible. They return the empty dishes with pieces of thread for long life, and rice and money for wealth. Red bean rice cakes are placed at the north, south, east, and west points of the house to scare off evil spirits.

Long-life noodles

The Chinese believe that eating long noodles on your birthday will bring you a long life. It is even luckier if you cook them without breaking them, and unlucky if you cut a strand.

Mouse biscuits

When a baby is born in The Netherlands, visitors are given "beshcuit met muisjes" ("little mice biscuits") to eat. These are round pieces of baked bread topped with butter and sugar-coated **aniseeds**. The aniseeds are pink and white for a girl, and blue and white for a boy. The biscuits are said to get their name because the seeds look like tiny mice.

If a royal baby is born, the aniseeds on little mice biscuits are orange, the color of the Dutch royal family.

Call to Prayer

The first words that a **Muslim** baby hears are those of a prayer. The father or grandfather whispers them in the baby's ear. The words are:

"**Allah** is great.

I bear witness that there is no God but Allah

I bear witness that Muhammad is the messenger of Allah.

Come to prayer

Come to safety

Allah is the greatest."

Something sweet, such as honey or a date, is placed on the baby's tongue to show the sweetness of leading a good life.

This Muslim father is whispering the words of the prayer into his baby's ear.

14

The baby is being blessed with holy water during the feast of Aqiqah.

Aqiqah ceremony

When the baby is seven days old, the family holds the Aqiqah ceremony to thank Allah for the baby's birth. Prayers are said to Allah and the baby's head is shaved. The hair is weighed, and the family gives the same weight in gold (or money) to charity. The baby is also given its name. Afterward, there is a feast for friends and neighbors.

MUSLIM NAMES

Muslim boys are usually named after the **Prophet Muhammad** or are given one of the 99 names of Allah. Muslim girls are named after members of Muhammad's family or other women mentioned in the Qur'an, the Muslim holy book.

Sitting in a Cradle

An ancient celebration, called Sebou, takes place in Egypt when a baby is seven days old. This is the time when friends and family visit to welcome the baby into the world.

At Sebou, the baby is carried around the house in a special cradle.

NAME CANDLES

At Sebou, the baby's name may be chosen by giving names to several different candles. The candles are lit at the start of the ceremony. The baby is named after the candle that burns for the longest time.

These children are holding name candles for a baby's Sebou ceremony in Egypt.

The ceremony begins with guests scattering salt around the baby's mother and the house to scare off evil spirits. The baby is bathed and dressed in new clothes. Then the baby is placed in a large cradle with a drain in it and taken on a tour of its home. It is followed by a procession of friends and relatives, carrying candles and singing songs.

Once the tour is over, the baby is shaken gently to prepare it for the ups and downs of life. The mother then steps over the baby seven times without touching him or her, while everyone else shouts and makes a lot of noise. This helps to get rid of evil spirits and also gets the baby used to hearing loud sounds.

Being Baptized

A few months after a **Christian** baby is born, he or she is taken to church to be **baptized**. A service is held at which the baby is accepted into the Christian faith and given a name. The baby's parents ask some close friends or relatives to be **godparents**. The godparents promise to help the baby to lead a good Christian life.

In church, the parents and godparents stand near the **font**. The font is a special container that is filled with holy water. The priest pours some of the water over the baby's head and makes the sign of the cross on his or her forehead. The water is meant to wash away sins. The cross is a symbol of Christianity.

This Christian baby is being baptized with holy water from a font.

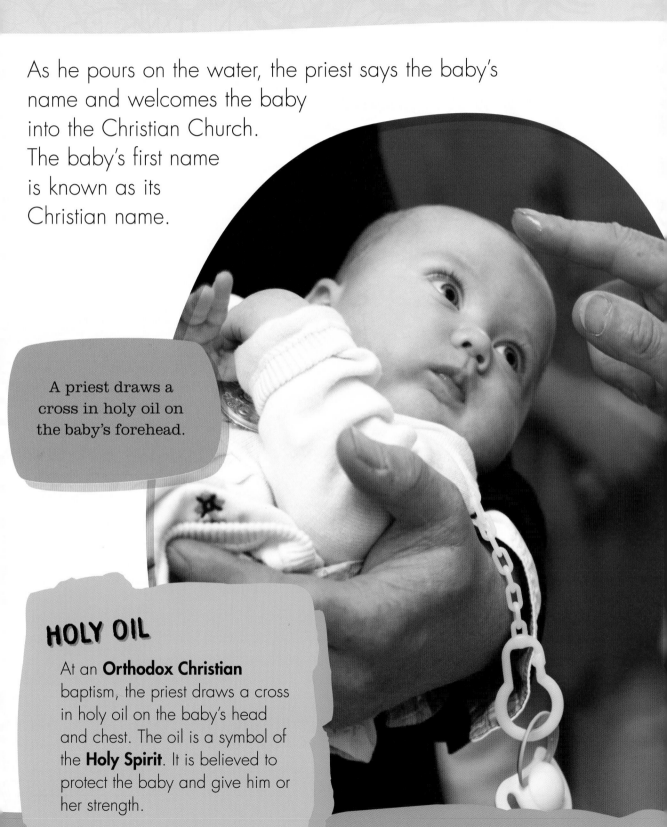

As he pours on the water, the priest says the baby's name and welcomes the baby into the Christian Church. The baby's first name is known as its Christian name.

A priest draws a cross in holy oil on the baby's forehead.

HOLY OIL

At an **Orthodox Christian** baptism, the priest draws a cross in holy oil on the baby's head and chest. The oil is a symbol of the **Holy Spirit**. It is believed to protect the baby and give him or her strength.

Inuit
Names

Inuit babies are often named after their grandparents.

The Inuit people live in the far north of Canada, Greenland, and Alaska. When an Inuit baby is a few days old, he or she is given an atiq (say "a-TEEK"), or "name-soul." This is usually the name and spirit of an older relative who has died. It is believed that the name will bring the personality of the relative to the child.

CHOOSING AN ATIQ

There are different ways to find the best atiq for a baby. The baby's mother might have a dream about a relative and choose his or her name-soul for her baby. A baby may have a **birthmark** in the same place as a relative—a sign that the baby is carrying on the relative's soul.

The Inuit believe that every living thing has a soul. When a person dies, his or her soul starts another life in a new person. This is called **reincarnation**. So, a baby not only gets his or her relative's name, but also that person's soul. After the atiq ceremony, the baby has a special link to the relative and tries to be like the relative as he or she grows up.

The Inuit believe that the reason some newborn babies cry a lot is because they want a particular atiq. Once a baby is given the right atiq, he or she will stop crying.

This Inuit mother is carrying her baby on her back.

Seeing the Sun

The Hopi people from the southwest United States hold a special naming ceremony when a baby is 20 days old. Until that time, the baby is kept indoors and does not see the sun.

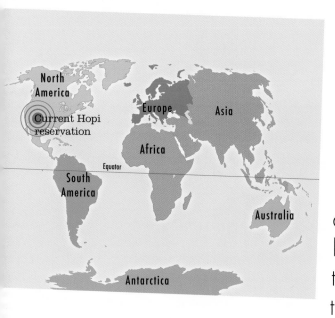

Early in the morning, before dawn, the baby is bathed and wrapped in a blanket. **Cornmeal** is rubbed in his or her hair. To the Hopi, corn is a symbol of life. Then, the baby's grandmother takes the baby outside, just as the sun is rising. She holds the baby up to the sun and calls out his or her name. She says a prayer over some cornmeal and rubs it on the baby's lips.

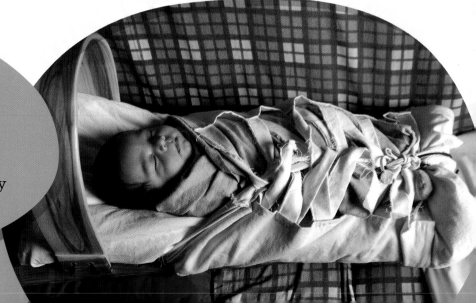

This Hopi baby is wrapped tightly in blankets and is sleeping on a back board. The board is used to carry the baby on the parent's back.

Tihu dolls are used to teach children about the katsinas (spirits).

After the naming ceremony, everyone gathers for a feast. They eat a special stew, made from corn and lamb, with blue cornbread and sweet cornmeal pudding. A small plate of food is placed on the floor by the door to give thanks to the earth.

TIHU DOLLS

When a baby is born, he or she is given a wooden doll called a tihu. The doll is said to be a gift from the katsinas. They are spirits that the Hopi believe live in everything in the world.

Happy Birthday, Everyone!

Tet is the Vietnamese New Year, which is celebrated in January or February. It is also the day on which everyone celebrates their birthday. Babies are said to turn one on Tet, no matter when they are actually born.

Altars like this one are set up in honor of people's ancestors.

Special Earth and sky cakes are offered to the ancestors at Tet.

A few days before Tet, people buy new clothes and clean their homes. This marks a new start and gets rid of bad luck. They decorate their homes with flowers, such as marigolds, which stand for long life.

TET TREES

Each family puts up a Tet tree, decorated with greetings cards and red charms. The tree might be a **kumquat** tree, with small, orange fruit, or a mail tree, with lucky yellow flowers.

Celebrations last for three days. On the first morning, children are given gifts of money in lucky red envelopes. This is also the day for visiting family. People set up **altars** in their homes and leave offerings of different types of fruit. These are in honor of their dead **ancestors** whom they believe visit during Tet.

Special cakes are made from sticky rice, beans, and pork wrapped in large, green leaves and steamed. Square cakes are symbols of Earth; round cakes are symbols of the sky. These are offered to the ancestors.

Birthday Fun Around the World

Birthday cakes

In many countries in North America and Europe, people celebrate their birthdays with a special cake. It is decorated with candles, one for each year of their age. While everyone sings "Happy Birthday to You," the birthday person blows out the candles and makes a wish.

In Russia, people have a fruit pie instead of a cake. A birthday message is pricked into the crust. Chinese people eat birthday pastries shaped like peaches. In Chinese cultures, peaches stand for long life.

What do you think these children are wishing for as they blow out the candles?

Party games

Every birthday party needs good party games. In the United Kingdom, friends give the birthday person something called "the bumps." You get lifted high into the air, then bumped on the ground, once for each year of your age, and once for luck.

In Mexico, a piñata is hung from the ceiling. The piñata is a large paper bag, sometimes shaped like an animal, and filled with toys, candy, coins, and candles. Sometimes each child is blindfolded and tries to knock the piñata down with a stick. Then they smash it open to get the goodies inside.

Happy birthday to you!

The famous "Happy Birthday to You" song was written by two American sisters, Mildred and Patty Hill, in 1893. It was originally called "Good Morning to All."

Make a Hopi Cradle Doll

Newborn Hopi babies are given flat tihu called "cradle dolls" (see page 23). These are usually carved from tree roots. You can recycle an old box to make colorful tihu dolls of your own.

- cardboard
- scissors
- ruler
- white glue
- feathers, felt, ribbon, or tissue paper
- paints
- black felt-tip pen

1 Cut out a rectangle of cardboard measuring 7 x 2.5 inches (18 x 6 cm).

2 Cut the end off the rectangle a quarter of the way down. Trim the top corners of both pieces, to give them rounded ends.

3 Decide which katsina your doll will represent. Will it be an animal, with fur or feathers? Will it be a person, with hair and ears?

4 Decorate the head using felt, tissue paper, feathers, or ribbon. Cut out shapes and glue them to the rounded end of the long piece of cardboard.

5 Glue the short piece of cardboard over the long piece, like a sandwich.

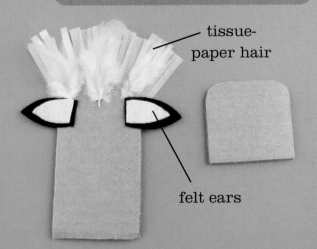

tissue-paper hair

felt ears

6 When the glue is dry, you can paint your tihu. Start with a coat of white paint. Add patches of bright color.

Don't let a baby play with your homemade tihu. Hang it on a wall like the Hopi do, so the baby can enjoy looking at it.

7 When the paint is dry, use a black felt-tip pen to add details.

Glossary

Allah Islamic name for God, in the Arabic language

altar place where offerings such as food and flowers are made to gods and ancestors

ancestor relative from the past

aniseed tiny black seed that tastes like licorice

baptized when a person has taken part in a ceremony to become a full member of the Christian church

birthmark dark mark on a baby's skin

Christian person who follows the Christian religion

cornmeal flour made from dried and ground-up corn

font container in a church that is filled with holy water

godparent person who promises to help raise a child as a good Christian

granthi Sikh who looks after and reads from the Guru Granth Sahib

gurdwara Sikh place of worship

Hindu person who follows the Hindu religion

Holy Spirit for Christians, one of the three ways of seeing God, as God's power working in the world

horoscope chart showing the position of the stars and planets at the time of a baby's birth

humanist person who does not believe in God but rather in people's actions

karma person's actions, good and bad, and their results

kumquat small, orange fruit that grows on a tree

mandir Hindu place of worship, sometimes called a temple

Muslim person who follows the religion of Islam

Orthodox Christian member of the Orthodox group of Christians

Prophet Muhammad last and greatest in a line of messengers sent by Allah to teach people how to live in the Muslim religion

reincarnation belief that a person is born again after he or she dies

semolina rough, pale-yellow flour ground from wheat

Sikh person who follows the Sikh religion

Find Out More

Books

Jones, Aled. *What Do You Believe?: Religion and Faith in the World Today*. New York: Dorling Kindersley, 2011.

Meredith, Susan. *The Usbourne Encyclopedia of World Religions* (Internet-Linked Encyclopedias). Tulsa, OK.: EDC, 2010.

Rohr, Ian. *Religious Celebrations* (Celebrations). Mankato, MN.: Smart Apple Media, 2011.

Web sites

Facthound offers a safe, fun way to find Internet sites related to this book. All of the sites on Facthound have been researched by our staff.

Here's all you do:

Visit www.facthound.com

Type in this code: 9781410980205

Further research

When is your birthday? How do you celebrate? Can you find out more about how people celebrate birthdays around the world? Which special food do they eat? Which birthday games do they play? You can look in books or on the Internet, or ask your friends.

Index